Donated By

Gerald Nestor
JAN 1991

HANG GLIDING

HANG GLIDING

by Dorothy Childers Schmitz

Copyright © 1978 by Crestwood House, Inc. All rights reserved. No part of this book may be reproduced in any form without written permission from the publisher, except for brief passages included in a review. Printed in the United States of America. Reprinted 1978, 1979

Library of Congress Catalog Card Number: 78-6200

International Standard Book Numbers:
0-913940-94-1 Library Bound
0-89686-015-9

Edited by - Dr. Howard Schroeder
    Prof. in Reading and Language Arts
    Dept. of Elementary Education
    Mankato State University

Library of Congress Cataloging in Publication Data

Schmitz, Dorothy Childers.
  Hang Gliding.

  (Funseekers)
  SUMMARY: A brief introduction to the equipment, techniques, and thrill of hang gliding.
   1. Hang gliding--Juvenile literature. (1. Hang gliding)
I. Schroeder, Howard. II. Title.
GV764.S35   797.5'5   78-6200
ISBN 0-913940-94-1

PHOTO CREDITS

George Uveges: 3, 11, 12, 15, 18, 20, 21, 24-25, 27, 31
Focus On Sports: Cover, 4, 17, 19, 28-29
Catherine Buckley, The Alberta Hang Gliding Assoc.: 6-7, 13
The Bettman Archives: 8, 9
Randall A. Conner: 14
Pete Hornby: 23, 32
Wills Wing Inc.: 26

HANG GLIDING

You stand there, waiting your turn. "The wind is right, isn't it?" The breeze catches you and your harness as you run through all the last minute checks. All eyes are on you. There is no backing out now. You hear the instructor shout that same order you have heard everyday of your training. But this time it's different. Very different. "Run! Run! Run!" You run into the wind, faster, faster, faster. The ground is no longer under you. You are flying!

Legendary Icarus takes to the sky.

Ever since man first watched birds fly overhead, he has wanted to fly. There is a legend about a man named Daedalus and his son, Icarus, who tried to fly. They tried to copy the way birds flew by making feathers into man-sized wings. They attached the wings with wax. The legend says that Icarus flapped the wings and flew. His father called out to warn him not to fly too close to the sun. But Icarus was too joyful to listen. He flew very close to the sun. The wax on the wings melted and Icarus fell to the sea.

The story of Daedalus and Icarus is just a legend. But for centuries, real men have wanted to fly. They have tried many different ways to fly like the birds they watched in the sky.

Leonardo da Vinci was one of those men. More than four hundred years ago, he drew plans for wings that he thought would fly. No one ever tried the wings. But other men through the years have made their own and have tried them. Some of them have died trying to fly. One of them was Otto Lilienthal. He fell during a test flight of one of his designs and broke his back. Before he died he told his friends that it was worth it to fly.

Otto Lilientahl's first experiments with a glider in 1891. He conducted his flight from an artificially made hill in the neighborhood of Berlin. During one of his attempts to extend the length of his flight over 350 yards he crashed fatally on August 9, 1896.

Other men kept working on what they called gliders. Even the Wright brothers, who later invented the airplane, first worked with man-powered gliders. Like flying, gliding has come a long way since those days. It has become a popular sport. Training schools have been set up for people who want to learn to hang glide safely. There are companies that make hang gliders in many patterns and colors. Hang gliders range in price from one hundred dollars for an unfinished kit, to a thousand dollars or more for a completed glider.

Most people think of danger when they think of hang gliding. They want to know, "Is it a safe sport?" The answer to that question depends on how you go about it. Anyone who wants to, can hang glide. A person can make a glider out of almost anything, jump off a cliff, and hope to land safely below. However, the person who wants to live to enjoy the sport will go about it the right way.

Proper training is important before trying to hang glide. There is a safe way to do almost everything. People do get killed hang gliding. Some of them were trained and still made a mistake which cost them their lives. Many glider accidents have been caused by a pilot's mistake. What can be learned by such accidents? The more training you get, the safer hang gliding can be.

Let's say that you are going to one of the many training schools around the country. What will they teach you? From the very beginning, they will teach you safety. The experts know, better than anyone else, how dangerous hang gliding is for a person without proper training. They would like to see that everyone who tries hang gliding has lessons in safety. People, who try it without understanding the sport, risk their lives. They also give the sport a bad name. People read about hang gliding accidents and they think of it as a dare-devil sport. There have been tradgedies. Many of them would not have happened if the fliers had known more about the sport.

Flying double is twice as exciting.

Throughout the course, you will be taught how to fly safely. You will begin by learning how to put your glider together. Fastening the bolts and securing all wires properly are very important. If your equipment is faulty, it may not matter what you know or don't know as you take off.

Next you will learn how to prepare for take-off. You have to learn how to balance your weight while holding your control bar. The control bar looks like a large triangle. It is the key to taking you where you want to go, and keeping you away from dangerous areas such as the ocean or back into the cliff!

You will also be taught how to adjust the straps and harnesses that hold you securely while gliding.

It is important to learn how to judge the wind. Knowing when to take off is just as important as knowing what to do when you are gliding. You should know about the conditions of your landing spot as well as the area from which you begin your flight. You will learn how to gauge the wind by the way the sail looks and sounds as you take off.

Experience is the key. You will have many practice runs on the ground without really taking off. By the time you make that first flight, you will have been to the edge of that running hill many times!

One of the most exciting parts of the training is learning how to run at top speed. This is what makes the glider lift you off the ground. It isn't as easy as it looks to run at top speed with the glider strapped on your back. You will be getting into good shape while you are training for this exciting sport.

Learning what to do after you are in the air comes next. You might wonder, "How can you practice the flying part?" If you're practicing it, you're doing it. At the training schools, a simulator is used to help you prepare for this sport. This is a frame that holds you in your control bar off the ground. It gives you the feel of what gliding will be like. The simulator can put you into a dive or stall. You must learn what to do when these things happen. If you don't, you won't be allowed to get into a real glider. You may not have another chance to learn if you don't know what to do during a real flight.

After you have learned these things at ground school, you are ready for flight school. This is the closest thing to a real flight. Your instructor takes you to a beginner hill. There you will set up your own glider, just the way you learned to do at ground school. Then you will put yourself into the harness, put on your helmet, and actually fly for the first time. It's just a beginner hill, but you are in the air. After all, that's what gliding is all about!

Now you have graduated from the "bunny hills" to the intermediate slopes. Here you will practice all the things you have been taught in ground school and on the bunny hill. You are getting ready for the cliffs and real flying.

More safety will be stressed. You will be told to check your glider after every landing. Some landings damage the glider even when the pilot is fine. You will check for such things as bent bolts, damage to the control bar, or rips in the sail. Some of these things can be taken care of on the spot. Other problems will have to wait to be sent away for repairs. No flier eager to learn ever welcomes the delay, but better delay than risk injury.

A folded down hang-glider is easy to transport.

You can't be too careful; check and recheck everything.

A story is told about a hang-glider pilot who noticed a stripped bolt on his glider. His buddy told him he should replace it right away. "One more flight," he said. "Then I'll quit for the day." Because of that damaged bolt, the wing broke on his next flight. The young pilot was killed. That was an accident that should not have happened. It is because of things like this that safety is so important.

Finally you are ready for the cliffs. However, this is not the end of the safety training. A sensible flier will learn from every flight. He will become not only a better pilot with every flight, but also a safer one.

What can you do with hang gliding besides enjoy yourself on Sunday afternoon? Sooner or later, you will probably want to get into a contest. The sport has come so far in the last few years that contests have become common. Before 1970 there were not as many as one hundred hang gliders all over the world. Now there are more than that in the air in a single afternoon in some popular spots around the country! There are associations for hang gliders to join which hold contests. The Southern California Hang Gliding Association began with only twenty-five members in 1971. It has become the United States Hang Gliding Association, Inc. with more than 7,000 members. Another association in California has more than 13,000 members. This association sends out newsletters to their members telling about contests. Whole families get involved in the sport. At some of the contests, the spot looks more like a campground with all the contestants, their families, and people who come to watch.

Interest in hang gliding is high in almost every state. People in other countries have become interested, too. Canada, Mexico, South America, Russia, Australia, and many other countries have organizations and contests. There is a magazine for hang gliders in Canada called *The Flypaper*. With so much interest in the sport, it was only natural that the contests and competitions developed into world championships.

Bob Wills.

The very first World Hang Gliding Champion was Greg Mitchell. The meet was held in 1973 at Sylmar, California. Since that first competition, many new ways of judging the pilots have been developed. Prizes now amount to thousands of dollars. Pilots are scored on safety, accuracy, turning ability, and grace. The 1975 U.S. champion, Bob Wills, was pushed all the way by his brother, Chris. He finished with 1,774 points out of a possible 2,000. One of the judges said, "Only a bird could have scored 2,000."

Some of the records have been set by accident. Reggie Miller of Berkeley, California set out to explore some good jumping sites. He found one he liked in Nevada. It was a 2,000-foot hill. He tried it and this is how he told friends about it:

"Have you ever seen a small piece of paper in the wind change its position several times, up and down, round and round in several seconds? That's what this ride was all about because I was caught in the wake of a high wind . . . I gained altitude quickly and it took me a full minute before I could land on the ridge to my left and only half-way down the mountain. On the way down I experienced free fall, almost hitting my head on the keel boom, and almost falling through the control bar. It was real terror! The minute lasted a full hour, and I quivered for five minutes. Ahhh, Mother Earth."

What do some of the champions say about hang gliding at its best? Taras Kickeniuk says "It's a kick to hang glide. You're all alone up there, not enclosed in a cockpit as you are in a sailplane, but out in the open. That has to be the closest thing to bird flight. It has to be. Just you and the wind in the wires."

Pete Brock tells about meeting a sea gull one day. "He came over to look me over. He came alongside as I was hovering. Neither of us moved. We were side by side studying each other. There wasn't a sound. I could see the slightest motion of the feathers at the end of his wings . . . I was thrilled."

Maybe it was an eighty-year-old grandmother who said it best. After her first flight, she said, "It was so exciting. Oh, it was just grand, simply wonderful. As soon as the glider is fixed, I'm going to go again."

If you decide to join the thousands who enjoy hang gliding, remember - a good pilot is a safe pilot. Stay smart and act wisely so that you will be around to enjoy the sport when you are eighty years old! It's great to be able to say, "I'm going to do it again!"

"I WANT TO FLY LIKE AN EAGLE
LET MY SPIRIT CARRY ME!"

LOCUST GROVE ELEM. LIBRARY

DATE DUE
NOV 29 1995
JAN 10 1996
APR 29 1996
MAY 8 1996
MAY 16 1996